WESTERN
WRITERS SERIES
No. 100

CAROL RYRIE BRINK

by Mary E. Reed

BOISE STATE UNIVERSITY
BOISE, IDAHO

Boise State University Western Writers Series   Number 100

Carol Ryrie Brink

By Mary E. Reed
Latah County Historical Society

Editors: Wayne Chatterton
James H. Maguire

Business Manager:
James Hadden

Cover Design and Illustration
by Arny Skov, Copyright 1991

Boise State University, Boise, Idaho

Library of Congress Card No. 91-55034

International Standard Book No. 0-88430-099-4

Printed in the United States of America by
Boise State University Printing and Graphics Services
Boise, Idaho

Carol Ryrie Brink

Carol Ryrie Brink

For a gifted storyteller with the ability to pluck the extraordinary from the ordinary, the occasion of Carol Ryrie Brink's birth would give her the opportunity to introduce herself into a particular place and time. Her life tentatively began on 28 December 1895. She grew up hearing the story of that winter evening from her grandmother until it became her own. Her grandfather, Dr. William W. Watkins, arrived at the Ryries' house on a sleigh pulled through the snow by his high-stepping horse. As the doctor pumped the baby's small arms up and down and blew his tobacco-scented breath into the cold, still body, an anxious father and exhausted mother waited to hear the thin cry. As Brink tells in her reminiscences, "I gave a sharp cry and began what has been a marvelous and rewarding journey, a thing too precious to be minimized, my lovely life" (*Chain of Hands* 6).

The world she entered was a modest house in Moscow, Idaho, the seat of a rural county in the northern part of the state. It boasted the distinction of having the state university, and although isolated, Moscow was firmly connected with the outside world by the new railroad. Living in Moscow her junior year at the University of Idaho gave Brink an intimate knowledge of this crucial period of development. Her youthful years spanned the settlement years of rustic one-story, wood-frame buildings lining Main Street to an era of paved roads and automobiles. In between, the pace was measured by foot or horseback, Main Street was the center of business and commerce, and social and cultural life firmly clung to church and civic clubs.

Brink entered this small-town Western scene as the youngest member of a well-respected family. William W. Watkins was a popular physician with a domineering personality who, as his granddaughter remembered him, was someone people either liked or disliked. As Brink describes him, "He was a big man with dark handle-bar moustaches. In his photographs he has a fierce and angry look. He was used to getting what he wanted . . . . Proud, confident, dynamic, single-purposed . . ." (*Chain* 50). After practicing medicine in Missouri and Kansas, he moved his family to Moscow in 1887.

In Moscow Dr. Watkins became a pillar of the community, distinguishing himself by helping to secure the state university and serving as regent. He was prominent in the Masons, owned property, and was, in short, symbolic of the new Western opportunist.

The other dominant male figures in Brink's early life were her father, Alexander Ryrie, and his brother Donald. There were four of these Scottish brothers who came to Moscow; one returned to Scotland. The gentle-natured Alexander worked for a large Scottish life insurance firm. He also served as mayor, surveyed the city streets, and taught Sunday School at the Presbyterian Church. The more aggressive Donald speculated in real estate and irrigation projects and lived a faster pace. A third brother, Henry, was considerably more carefree and less successful. This variety of avuncular personalities assuredly helped form Carol Brink's healthy attitude toward men and marriage.

Brink's mother, Henrietta, was a beautiful and emotional woman, a gifted musician but as her daughter remembers, not very interested in being a mother. Brink admitted that at the time of her mother's death she possessed few memories of this mysterious woman. As she grew older, Brink became convinced that her mother had little love for her. In fact, the emotional ties between mother and daughter were so lacking, that Brink poignantly re-counts one instance when a strange young woman gave her a great warmth and tenderness she had wanted but had not re-ceived from her own mother. In later years she was able to fit this isolated piece into a wider perspective. "For, though my mother must have fondled me and taken me upon her lap or held me in her arms or even lain beside me on a bed a great many times in the eight years we were together, I cannot remember one of them. There must have been in her embrace something perfunctory and unfelt; a duty done toward a little, homely child who did not oc-cupy the center of her heart" (*Chain* 25). It was important to her writing career that she was able to overcome this emotional depri-vation.

Brink's grandmother, Caroline Watkins, amply provided the ma-ternal bond. Prevented by her parents from marrying her first love, she married the young Doctor. Of their eight children, three died in infancy. At her husband's death, she found herself with a lapsed insurance policy, rundown property, a stack of unpaid bills, and a grandchild to rear. Fortunately she possessed the inner re-sources that allowed her to sustain her losses and was able to pass on to the young Brink the lessons not only of accepting life as it comes but also of stability, security, wisdom, and good sense. Her influences shaped Brink's life and writing into an optimistic and realistic harmony. Brink admits that her grandmother crept into nearly every book she wrote, sometimes as the chief character, sometimes with a minor part, and sometimes merely by imbuing the book with her spirit (*Chain* 28 and 34).

Caroline Watkins also represented a romantic spirit because of her vivid memories of a childhood on the Wisconsin frontier. Her stories about her childhood greatly influenced the genesis of Brink's writing career, for they gave the child a sense of continuity with the past. Gram's life offered a wonderful, peaceful contrast between the childhood—which Brink immortalized in *Caddie Woodlawn* in the tomboy who befriended the Indians and scandalized the circuit rider—and the quiet old woman who seldom left the house, whose interests were not broad, and whose opinions were not unusual.

Brink's aunts, Elsie and Winifred, also influenced her life and works. Elsie was a complicated person who, frustrated by her father's refusal to let her become a nurse, lived at home most of her adult life. After Brink's mother died, Elsie took over Carol's upbringing with an engulfing devotion. This affection and dedication threatened to possess her, but fortunately she was able to nourish a small seed of individuality that kept her "from being completely her thing." It was Aunt Elsie who shared the young Carol's bedroom, making her room comfortable and placing a protective arm around her in the bed they shared. Eventually Brink asserted her independence and Aunt Elsie moved downstairs, greatly hurt by this act of rebellion from her niece (*Chain* 36).

Elsie also provided a lesson in the complexities of women "caught between the pruderies of Victoria and the freer thinking of the Edwardians." Although she had an unbridled tongue and frequently made indiscreet, shocking remarks, inside she was "completely virginal," and "horrified by license in other people" (*Chain* 19).

Winifred was a disruptive element, a wild card. Brink admits she spent most of her life disliking her Aunt Win. Like Henrietta, Winifred was temperamental and a talented musician, but unlike her older sister, she was lazy, self-centered, and lacking in responsibility. She was her father's favorite, and at the time of his death, Winifred was "a little red-haired girl of twelve" prepared to violently rebel against her mother. Having witnessed many painful scenes between Winifred, Elsie, and Caroline, Brink determined to avoid this chaos in her own life.

When Winifred was sixteen, she eloped with a man twice her age. Returning for a brief period to Moscow, Winifred found an appropriate outlet for her great vitality by becoming the accompanist for the local movie house. When she tired of this occupation, she left her husband and two sons to run away with a handsome doctor. She left her two young boys in the capable hands of Caroline Watkins. Communications from Winifred, who changed her name to Wanda, were scarce, but "they nearly always ended on the same note, a plea for money" (*Chain* 45).

Winifred died in poverty, but her influence persisted in Brink's novels. The author's initial sense of outrage mellowed into acceptance and an attempt to understand the complexities of this restless woman. This was an important healing process because it allowed Brink to use Winifred's character in many novels without moralizing or creating a stereotype.

The series of events which destroyed Brink's secure childhood world spanned a brief three years from her fifth to her eighth year. Alexander Ryrie died of consumption in July 1900. The next year, on 4 August 1901, a crazed gunman murdered William Watkins. Although Brink was not as emotionally attached to her grandfather as to her grandmother, his death brought the reality of violence into her early life. Because she grew up with the accounts of the murders and of the crazed gunman's death after a two-hour gun battle with a posse, Brink realized how such incidents become an integral part of a town's communal memory. The incident posed questions of justice and mob action in a small Western town, questions that she would explore in *Buffalo Coat*.

These deaths were followed by one of greater personal consequence. After Alexander's death, Henrietta married Nat Brown, the son of a prominent timber buyer. Brown had made some fast, lucrative deals with the Weyerhaeuser timber concerns, and he was, according to Brink, more interested in social pleasures than family responsibilities, particularly those concerning his shy and plain stepdaughter. In *Snow in the River*, Brink admits a distaste for this man, an aversion which increased rather than diminished with time (167). During this period Brink found solace in her grandmother's house. Although the memory of her stepfather was one of distaste, she admitted that "It must be difficult for a man to love a former husband's child, especially if that child is silent and resentful" (177). Henrietta and Nat Brown became part of Moscow's faster social set, and Brink describes him as a man who drank too much, used profanity, and fought with her mother.

The marriage added another layer of gossip onto the Watkins household. Henrietta's suicide in 1904 was the outcome of this desperate unhappiness, leaving Carol an orphan and in the care of her grandmother and her spinster aunt. No one told Brink the circumstances of her mother's death until she was eighteen or nineteen; by then it was neither a shock nor a surprise, "but only a rude bringing into the open of what had been tacitly understood" (*Chain* 23). The description of the chilling numbness she felt at her mother's death is one of Brink's best written passages, and she describes herself as a cold and quiet little girl, dry eyed and grim (*Snow* 189-90).

After the suicide, Donald Ryrie asked the three Watkins women to come to Spokane and keep house for him. For Brink, it was an idyllic existence, because Ryrie enjoyed buying her expensive gifts and showing her off to his friends. This happy interlude abruptly ended when he remarried. The three women moved back to Moscow to the Watkins' large home, but there they had to face a final scandal with Ryrie's bankruptcy.

In Moscow Brink was remembered as a shy, nice girl, unremarkable except for her pony and pony cart. The family's economic and social situation had abruptly changed, and they entered "the next level of caste, the unsung middle class who attended to business but rarely went out socially" (*Chain* 80-81).

Yet the experience of being an orphan and often lonely had a positive influence on Brink's creativity. The quiet of her grandmother's house trained her to create her own amusements. The childhood hours spent painting and drawing, reading and riding into the Idaho countryside, inspired her determination to write and illustrate her own books.

Although Brink's inheritance from her father was modest, it provided sufficient funds to see her through college. It also became an important emotional link to her father. She grew up with "the confidence of a person of independent means. A generous allowance was doled out to me every week, and I knew that it came from my own money and that more was in the bank" (*Chain* 78).

Being a precocious child, Brink was aware that their family was different from others in Moscow, that something terrible and unspeakable had happened. Under these circumstances, her ability to face the world cheerfully was fortunate if not remarkable. Instead of being consumed with self-pity and fear, she concentrated on developing her inner resources. Her grandmother proved a valuable ally in this process. Gram passed along her innate storytelling abilities to her granddaughter.

Brink and her future husband, Raymond, had first met in 1909 when he, only nineteen years old, arrived in Moscow to teach at the University's prep school. He rented a spare room at the Watkins' large house and befriended the thirteen-year-old Carol. A quiet young man who had progressed rapidly and successfully through school without time for frivolity, he was too young to participate in his classmates' social life. "Blinky," as Raymond was nicknamed, became a member of the neighborhood bunch which included Caroline and Elsie Watkins, neighbors, and other young people. The age difference between Carol and Raymond may have delayed their ultimate attachment and marriage, but these years gave them an opportunity to become good friends. Raymond tutored Carol in mathematics and they invented elaborate codes which allowed them to communicate "shy and pleasant things" safe from Elsie's scrutiny (*Chain* 192).

Although Caroline Watkins approved of Raymond, Elsie became alarmed that her niece was slipping away from her. She was furious when Raymond confided at the end of his school term that he intended to marry Carol when she was older. After a summer of exchanging letters, Raymond returned to Moscow but took a room elsewhere. Elsie banned him from the Watkins house. Although the year began with an emotional separation between the couple, it ended with an understanding. The next year Raymond left to complete his studies at Harvard, and their relationship continued through letters.

After Raymond left Moscow, Elsie persuaded the family to move to Portland, Oregon, for Brink's last two years of high school in the Portland Academy. Stricken with homesickness, Brink lived in her aunt and grandmother's Portland apartment instead of boarding at the school. She took comfort in her diary and Raymond's faithful letters, and on Valentine's Day Raymond sent her the usual bouquet of pink carnations. Elsie was silent, but a few days later Brink found a letter from Elsie in her diary demanding that she end her relationship with him. Devastated by this intrusion into her private life, she felt she could never forgive her aunt, who was asking her "to give up one of the dear and human connections that I still had with the world." Still, she complied and sank into a terrible depression which she remembers as the lowest spot in her life, "and I was just sixteen" (*Chain* 196-97).

The next year Brink returned alone to the Portland Academy. As life became brighter, she resolved to resume her correspondence with Raymond after telling her aunt of her intention during the Christmas holidays (*Chain*, 197). This act of defiance finally released her from her aunt's domination. During the year she also conquered a debilitating shyness. When the school magazine printed one of her articles, she blossomed under the attention of the editor and admiration of her colleagues. With a new self-confidence she returned to Moscow and enrolled at the University of Idaho.

Her home town college was her second choice to Wellesley, which was beyond the means of her father's legacy. She joined a sorority and enthusiastically participated in college society. She was editor of the society page of the school newspaper and wrote skits for the class plays. After three years she felt a need to expand her knowledge of the world, so she completed her senior year at the University of California in Berkeley with a close friend from the University of Idaho, Nora Ashton. At Berkeley, Carol became engaged twice; Raymond traveled to France on a fellowship and had romances with two other girls. Their next meeting occurred that fall when he made a special trip to resume the courtship, and the following Christmas he proposed. Her engagement to Raymond foreshadowed a break with Moscow and Idaho that would be more complete than she had imagined or desired (*Chain* 199). Because Elsie had married the previous year, Brink hoped that she could be married in her grandmother's house, but Elsie bluntly forbade it. Out of a misguided sense of helping her niece or perhaps motivated from jealousy, she castigated Carol for jeopardizing a potential writing career with a premature marriage. Devastated by this petty decision, Brink left Moscow and Idaho to be married at the Brink's cabin at a Wisconsin lake. This time it was Elsie who cried and Brink who was happy to be done with the old life and make a new beginning. That beginning flourished in the warm and wide circle of her new family. Built on a long-nurtured friendship, mutual tastes, and respect, the Brinks' marriage was successful. With the happiness and fulfillment of her adult years, Carol's bitterness over her aunt's pettiness disappeared.

Carol and Raymond's lives evolved smoothly. He taught at the University of Minnesota for the next forty years while Carol enjoyed her role as a faculty wife, although she neglected her social duties for her family and writing. She joined the Faculty Women's Club and initiated a writers' section. Later she taught creative writing at Hamlin University. The Brinks' habits were mutually well-suited; both had careers that focused on writing, and there were always two desks at home and at hotels during their travels. Raymond also proved to be a good editor and critic.

The pleasures of marriage widened with the birth of two children, David and Nora, in 1919 and 1930. A second enriching experience was her husband's numerous sabbaticals and vacations in Europe. These experiences abroad added to her repertoire of materials for her books, but she never became a writer alienated or exiled from her roots. Her writing career began in a modest manner with numerous stories published in children's magazines. She had not anticipated writing juvenile fiction but was inspired to do so by her children. Writing was a compulsion, but to a woman who put family responsibilities foremost, this meant writing on the end of the ironing board or the kitchen table when the children were in bed or in school. Her rigorous schedule of writing each morning, leaving the afternoons free for family and personal affairs, was a balance that well-suited Brink.

Macmillan published her first children's book, *Anything Can Happen on the River*, in 1934. But winning the Newbery Award in 1936 for *Caddie Woodlawn*, published in 1935, gave her the self-confidence to continue writing. Along with winning immediate recognition as a serious writer, it provided money for household help, freeing her to begin work on her adult novels. Her relationship to Macmillan was mutually beneficial. Except for five juvenile books and a gothic romance she wrote "just for fun," Macmillan published all her works and encouraged her writing career. One exception was her last manuscript, "Chain of Hands," which they rejected. By then, there was a new editor and the relationship that had begun in the 1930s ended. In addition to receiving the Newbery Medal in 1936, Brink was honored with the Friends of American Writers Award in 1955 and an honorary degree of Doctor of Letters from the University of Idaho in 1965. In 1966 the National League of American Pen Women gave her its award for fiction.

For one year after Raymond's retirement, the Brinks lived in Florida, where he taught at the University at Coral Gables. Not liking the climate, they moved to La Jolla, California. When Raymond died in 1976, Carol moved to Wesley Palms, a retirement community in San Diego. After a career of twenty-seven books written for children and adults, Brink turned to poetry, painting, and friends to fill out her remaining years.

Brink was honest about her career and her stature as a writer. She candidly admitted that she had been lucky enough to have a small success in her career, and although she dreamt of becoming a great writer, she settled for much less than greatness. She avoided literary circles and celebrities. Having been snubbed herself, she resolved to be gracious to her own fans and fellow writers (Interview Tapes 5 and 2).

Near the end of her life, Brink expressed confidence that she had accomplished all that she had wanted as a writer. There were no unfinished books, great projects, or unhealed wounds. The things that burned to be said were written "in the burning days when I was young." In 1981 she sensed that her last project to write about her experiences in Scotland might never be finished and would probably not find a publisher (*Chain of Hands 92*; Interview Tapes 4 and 15). She died in August of that year, full of kindness, vigor, and a strong attachment to her Idaho roots.

Among her contributions to Western American literature is the work she wrote about Idaho as a native of the state. In view of the relatively few Idaho writers of this period, that is of interest in itself. But there are more important considerations. One is the portrayal of a West between two eras, when towns like Moscow accelerated toward becoming a replica of any small American town. This was the town-building period when women's groups brought to maturity churches and schools, libraries, parks, literary societies, and all the cultural developments of small-town life.

Brink brings to her writing an interpretation of her time period and her social class. She embodies a middle-class perspective of the 1940s and 1950s that avoided revealing personal hostility, bitterness, or alienation. Yet she is not prudish. She is able to weigh the values of respectable society with that same society's impulse to stifle and condemn the nonconformist. Her own social descent from being the mayor's daughter to being an orphan gave her a penetrating insight and empathy. She was a non-judgmental champion of decency while retaining a fascination with the daring, impatient, and rebellious women who wanted more than a good marriage and children. In Brinks' fiction they are neither scorned nor ridiculed, but neither are they accepted. As she admitted in an interview, writing about her mother in *Snow in the River* was therapeutic because it let her express the anguish she felt from her mother's death and because it allowed her to rid herself of some things that had bothered her all her life (Interview Tapes 4 and 11). Nonetheless, the novel, as did her life, avoids exploiting the personal events.

THE CHILDREN'S BOOKS

The classic children's book, *Caddie Woodlawn*, published in 1935, influenced Brink's career, which extended another thirty years. The book expresses Brink's philosophy of writing and her attitudes toward the values of the pioneer era.

Having grown up hearing pioneer stories from her grandmother, Brink was well acquainted with the subject matter for this book. It was in Paris with her husband after having completed her first children's book, *Anything Can Happen on the River* (1934), that Brink received a newspaper clipping from her grandmother. It described the death of "Indian John" at the age of 120 years, and Gram Watkins claimed that this was the same Indian she had known as a girl. The article flooded Brink's mind with the mass of stories and anecdotes which had lain beneath the surface for many years. She instantly knew that whatever fate was in store for *Anything Can Happen on the River*, she would write a book for children about Caddie.

The preparation would take over a year. As with all her books, Brink was concerned with recreating as accurately as possible the historical setting, including the small, everyday details. She sent long letters to her grandmother asking about the everyday details of the period, and she visited the Woodhouse homestead and other sites that would be in the book. The mass of stories and anecdotes took another year to sort out and put into a one-year chronology.

Caddie Woodlawn was an immediate success and a dark horse candidate for the Newbery medal. Winning the award launched Brink's career, giving her self-confidence to continue her writing career and recognition as a gifted children's author.

As a classic of children's literature, *Caddie Woodlawn* is widely remembered with great affection. One boyhood fan, Louie Attebery, editor of *Northwest Folklore*, recently described the book as an "artistic accomplishment of a high order" and "unfortunately labeled as juvenile." The greatest aspects of this art, Attebery suggests, are the skillful projection of Caddie from girlhood to becoming a young lady and the small details which provide "entry into a rich cultural matrix" of this pioneer world ("Another Look at

Caddie Woodlawn").

Caddie also reveals Brink's attraction to America's pioneer past, an attraction nurtured by the personal link with her grandmother. Brink feared that young Americans were losing the values of hard work, sacrifice, and idealism at a time when they needed courage, a willingness to meet the unknown, and steadfastness. The didactic purpose of her children's books, certainly more muted but still present in her adult fiction, reflected her conviction that children's literature should contain ideals as well as stimulate children through imaginative and honest writing. She advocated presenting great deeds and noble endeavors to children living in a contemporary world lacking in ideas and marked by disillusionment. Brink firmly believed that it was an author's duty to write as well for children as for adults (Interview Tapes 4 and 11).

Decades later, feminists criticized *Caddie* for what they claimed was a chauvinistic attitude. The kernel of their disapproval centered on a speech Caddie's father gives to his rambunctious daughter. The speech summarizes Brink's position on the women's question, a position which was both well-defined and flexible. "A woman's work is something fine and noble to grow up to, and it is just as important as a man's. But no man could ever do it so well. I don't want you to be the silly affected person with fine clothes and manners, whom folks sometimes call a lady . . . . I want you to be a woman with a wise and understanding heart, healthy in body and honest in mind" (240).

Even though Brink's life was a testimony to a woman having a meaningful career, it was accomplished as a compromise among duties of raising children, keeping house, and being a wife. Nonetheless, Brink felt that she always had a choice, and she grew up with the conviction that she could be anyone or do anything she wanted. As evidence of greater freedom for women in the West, she often pointed to the example of Idaho being among the first states to give women the vote. Yet this freedom of decision was not to be at the expense of family, and it becomes an important theme in many if not most of her adult novels.

THE IDAHO NOVELS

After writing *Caddie Woodlawn* and two other children's books, Brink wrote one of her best adult novels, *Buffalo Coat*. Published in 1944, it was based on her grandparents' lives but avoided sensitive material. Brink was not yet prepared to write about the events closest to her. *Buffalo Coat* is an excellent regional novel, with a universality of character and plot in the special setting of northern Idaho. The characters explore the theme of why people came to this small town she names Opportunity, the fictionalized name of Moscow. Brink interprets this migration primarily as a desire to escape the past and find a new life. The central character, Dr. Hawkins, is escaping from a mediocre career in the Midwest and from the death of his two sons. The Idaho West and the town of Opportunity give him the backdrop for playing a leading role. He becomes an important citizen, buys property, helps organize the new university, and is the town's leading physician. The excitement of building and creating something new, while also creating a monument for himself, is intoxicating. As he explains to his new assistant, "I'm building and that's why I came West where everything has to be done . . . . We're building for the future, for the boys and girls who are growing up, for the men and women of tomorrow. God, for the fun of building!" (33).

A second doctor in the novel, Constant Duvall, is an emigré from France who reflects the heterogeneous nature of new Western towns. Duvall's alcoholism caused the death of his wife during childbirth, and he has come to this part of America to try to escape his guilt. Through his character Brink refutes the stereotype of the West as a permanent refuge. For Duvall as for other newcomers, these places were only temporary. "Stop here until you can go backward," is the advice Duvall receives (419).

The third doctor, Hugh Allerton, is an Englishman. He moves to Opportunity to fulfill his career and forget his unhappy marriage to a frigid and reclusive wife. He learns that for those who come too late and challenge the existing order, there are insurmountable barriers. Hawkins, jealous of losing his primacy as the town's medical authority, tries to force him out. When Allerton falls in love with the young daughter of the Methodist minister, Hawkins is the unknowing instrument that forces the couple's suicide.

The fictional account is based on the actual occurrence which Brink grew up hearing as folklore. However, she rejects contemporary explanations that the doctor exerted hypnotic control over the young woman. Instead, she portrays two people caught in an impossible situation where the only resolution appeared to be ending their lives after spending one perfect day together.

Despite the strong male characters in the book, *Buffalo Coat* is clearly a woman's novel. It owes its force to the influence of Brink's grandmother and to what Brink knew about the sometimes quiet, behind-the-scenes accomplishments of women in Western communities. Anna Hawkins does not choose to move West but obediently follows her doctor husband. Although she accepts it as her duty, she also insists on defining her own life within these constraints. Doctor Hawkins would like to have a wife who entertains, dresses in conventional finery, and observes social customs. Anna firmly rejects these proddings. She has a larger perspective, sensing a danger surrounding these hastily constructed towns and societies. She attempts to communicate her fears to her husband: "We don't half know this place, Doctor . . . . All this building and planning, all the bustles and high hats and making social calls and going to church—that's not really Opportunity." Doctor impatiently asks, "Then what in tarnation is,

Anna? We're building something here." "Yes, you're building something, but it won't be finished for a long time. You've put a thin crust of civilization over the pie, but crack the surface anywhere and it's still bear meat and venison underneath" (21-22).

The savageness of the American West in *Buffalo Coat* arises not only from an eruption of vengeance but also from ignorance about mental illness. The character of Alf Stevens explores the consequences of violent acts. Alf's father committed suicide when he was young, and Alf becomes a public nuisance. He is even rumored to have beaten his mother. Dr. Hawkins signs the papers committing Alf to an institution, and when Alf is prematurely released, it is Dr. Hawkins who leads a deputation of leading citizens to warn him against further violence. By this time severely unbalanced, Alf rides through the streets on a Sunday morning, carrying a list of men he intends to murder. Dr. Hawkins is the first victim.

Following the actual scenario, the town organizes a posse which pursues Alf to his house on the outskirts of town. There they steadily barrage the house with gunfire until they are sure Alf is dead. In horror over the result of their actions, the posse conceals the fact that one of them has killed Alf; they attribute his death to suicide.

Anna is the rational counterpoint to this male violence. Despairing at her first view of Opportunity with its one-story wooden houses and muddy streets, she develops a mind rich in resources that keeps her company at lonely moments and learns how to accept things as they are and to compromise. The ability to compromise was a necessary trait for women like Anna who would not have come West on their own and who had to adjust to a new life without the friendships and family ties they had left behind.

Anna also represents the woman with roots in a pioneer era who cannot easily accommodate herself to a secondary role. She is skilled at repairs and knows how their rental property should be managed. When Anna suggests that they tear down the shacks and put up decent cottages designed the way a woman would like with cupboards and a copper sink, Doctor Hawkins admonishes her to leave the business end to him. "It takes a man to work a deal like this." Yet it is Anna who saves the family from her husband's improvident investments by saving money, cutting corners, and selling fruit, eggs, and chickens. She does this quietly, knowing he would be irritated with her petty economies (177-78).

Within this male-female tension, Brink skillfully brings the couple together with the reality of shared lives. After sustaining some personal and professional losses, Doctor Hawkins reflects on his life with Anna and his feelings toward her: "It was strange how he had always been with Anna. They lived so close, and he loved her more than he had ever loved any other woman, but still there were things that he never said to her . . . . Doc had never felt much need of women; he was a man's man, as they say. And yet where would he have been without Anna?" (399).

The strong, central female character of Anna is similar to those drawn by Willa Cather in her two novels, *O Pioneers* (1913) and *My Ántonia* (1918). Brink named Cather as one of the writers, along with Henry James, she most admired, and both Brink and Cather shared a common attachment to the Western landscape and fascination with its small-town society as reflected through women. In the two authors' novels of the Midwest and the West, women hold together the farms and families during the post-pioneer period of rapid growth and change. The central figure of *O Pioneers* is as strong as Anna Hawkins but possesses a mystical attachment to the land. Although the personalities of the two are different, one aggressive and one accepting, they share a bond with the land, looking to it for comfort and inspiration. A scene of Alexandra drawing comfort from the sky and the order of the stars foreshadows Anna's spiritual connection to the Idaho mountains. As Alexandra is fortified to reflect upon the great operations of nature, so, too, does Anna find peace in the serene, unchanging peaks of the mountains, which are the only permanence in her life (421).

Ántonia, like Anna, knits together the novel she appears in, *My Ántonia*, displaying a wisdom and fortitude lacking in the narrator, Jim Burden. Like Anna, Ántonia finds peace in work and within herself. Even though she becomes grizzled and battered by hard work and a hard life, she can "reveal the meaning in common things . . . . All the strong things of her heart came out in her body, that had been so tireless in serving generous emotions . . ." (353).

Buffalo Coat also explores the position of Western women through the character of Jenny Walden who is beautiful, energetic, and intelligent. Walden becomes a town heroine when she champions the town's fight for a modern sewage system, debating and defeating the powerful Doctor Hawkins.

A daughter of the poor Methodist minister, Walden has aspirations for an independent and meaningful life, but they appear doomed when her mother becomes seriously ill. It is her duty to stay home and give up plans to become a teacher. When the English doctor comes to treat her sprained ankle, Jenny finds a soulmate in this gentle man who reads poetry to her. Their infatuation and then love ends in a suicide pact.

Jenny Walden symbolizes the frustrations of poor—perhaps all—women of this era, and Brink balances the social injustice with the understanding of what was possible in the days before divorce and affairs were acceptable. In her reminiscence, "Chain of Hands," Brink remarks on how the affair might have been casually handled in contemporary times with a few weekends in a motel resolving the matter. Instead, Brink used the examples of these two lovers to lament the lack of moral depth in modern life, commenting that "genuine tragedy requires moral values. It requires virtue and sin and a sense of guilt. These things have very nearly been lost to us" (61).

Nonetheless, Brink avoids interpreting the relationship between the doctor and young woman as an example of small-town prejudice. She chooses to present the affair as a personal choice of two lovers who found the alternatives of divorce, living in sin, or giving each other up as unthinkable. The great harm they do is to innocent people. On the train returning from the scene of the suicide, Anna Hawkins tells Jenny's father that heaven and hell are within each person. "They've had their heaven, and less hell than they would have had if they had lived. They can sleep very quietly now and go back to earth whence they came" (303).

Buffalo Coat uses the landscape as a major theme, and Brink offers two perspectives. Although the landscape permeates Western American writing and dominates how Westerners identify themselves, the homesteaders often viewed it as a resource to be exploited or as posing obstacles to their human enterprises. While Brink celebrated the beauty and intrinsic values of the regional landscape, she was aware of how immigrants brought with them old patterns of living and thinking. Although Opportunity is on the outskirts of the mountains that rise toward the Continental Divide, most of the residents have turned away from the landscape. The French Doctor Duval remarks to himself how strange it was that the townspeople built so they did not look out at the mountains but faced their houses toward the streets. Instead of windows to the mountains, they put photographs of their families on the walls.

The landscape has a debilitating effect on the Stevens family. Alf's father lacks a vision of what the region can offer, and he is unable to adapt. He hangs himself ostensibly because of a bad crop and fights with his wife. But underneath he was a book-keeper from the East, expecting to get rich soon like the rest of the newcomers, and he "let his place go ragged when a little elbow grease might just have saved it" (16).

The reverse side of the alienation from the new land is a sense of spiritual values in the mountains and air. Through Anna, Brink uses the atmosphere of clear air in these high elevations to explain and anticipate the violence, "The feeling of threat, danger and strangeness." Like the main character in *O Pioneers*, Anna Hawkins uses the mountains as a reference point as her life changes. The novel ends with Anna contemplating the eternal paradox of the mountains. "Ever changing, now blue, now purple, now pale as silk; sometimes tremendous and threatening the sky, and sometimes dwindled to a gentle undulation around a peaceful valley, the mountains seemed as fickle as water; and yet they were the only permanence. In all of their variety, they were the only certain thing, the serene, unchanging peaks which rose above the quicksands of passing days and of humanity. And birth and death, and gain and loss, and even love itself, these were the shadows and the transiencies" (420-21).

Brink's Idaho novels also offer a perspective on the process of building a Western community. The main characters have arrived in Opportunity when it is a cluster of simple wooden buildings separated by muddy streets, but the novel's time frame extends through the rapid phase of replacing wood with brick, establishing a town elite society dominated by the new wealth of merchant families, and extending rudimentary education with a preparatory school for the new university. The Academy of Higher Learning expresses hope and civic pride, and for Dr. Hawkins, personal achievement. But there is about the process a self-consciousness which Brink skillfully captures. As she knew, the Intermountain West enjoyed priding itself on avoiding the wickedness of gold camps and outlaws. Building the Academy symbolized Opportunity's distance from the untamed and unlawful West. At the dedication of the Academy, Dr. Hawkins reminds his audience that some had been members of the vigilante committees in the south that captured and hanged men. "Those wild days of disorder are still fresh in our memories, but thank God, they are over and done with forever" (149). Declaring mob rule dead in Idaho, Hawkins congratulates the new pioneers who have stayed to put something into the state, instead of carrying it away on pack mules.

Opportunity also symbolizes a tension between the individual's authority and the impersonal, legal process. Hawkins has treated an Italian worker who murdered a man threatening his woman. The man escapes and Hawkins conceals the crime. When the man is captured, Hawkins is called to trial to defend his actions. Hawkins successfully does this by asserting his belief in individual justice, rejecting "the kind of justice that comes in wholesale lots." Yet some have their doubts that justice in Opportunity should turn on Dr. Hawkins' personal choices. The doctor who was responsible for uncovering Hawkins' deception contends that he has no quarrel with Dr. Hawkins. "I should have been sorry to see him tried and convicted; but there are principles which are more important than men . . . and someone in a town has to stand for those principles, even at the risk of making himself disliked" (240 and 245).

Buffalo Coat proved popular with critics and the public. Thelma Purtell, reviewing the novel in the *New York Times Book Review* (26 November 1944), described it as containing the right ingredients for a historical novel. She noted that the characters were timeless in their motivations, their emotions, their essential humanness, yet their destinies were molded and determined by the effect of a particular era and environment. The *Saturday*

Review of Literature (2 December 1944) also praised the novel as neither romanticizing nor vilifying small-town life, praising Opportunity and its characters as "living and credible creations."

Buffalo Coat was on the *Times* best seller list for two weeks. But with a paper shortage created by World War II, Macmillan chose to reprint the racier *Forever Amber* instead. When the second printing of *Buffalo Coat* finally appeared, the reviewers had lost interest.

After an interval of almost twenty years, Brink completed the second of her Idaho trilogy, *Strangers in the Forest*, published in 1959. The third Idaho novel, *Snow in the River*, appeared in 1964. Although the two novels round out Brink's Idaho experiences, *Strangers* is more a novel with only some use of biographical and personal information while *Snow in the River* is autobiographical to a large extent. *Strangers* also was a departure for Brink in that it required more research than her other novels, including the role of the Midwestern lumber barons.

Brink met one of the most famous of those barons when her mother entertained Frederick Weyerhaeuser and his sons at a dinner. Equally important to her early impressions of the beginnings of the lumber industry in north Idaho was Brink's stepfather, Nat Brown. Brown's father, C. O. Brown, persuaded Weyerhaeuser to inspect the white pine forests as a potential site for a logging operation. In addition, Alexander and Donald Ryrie and Brink's Aunt Elsie purchased timber holdings as speculative property. Elsie was only one of many Moscow women who filed these claims with the expectation that when they proved up they could sell the timber to waiting speculators. The issue was not as cold-blooded as it appeared. For women like Brink's aunt, this was one of the few ways open to single women to gain some financial independence. To them, the white pine was a symbol of both independence and natural beauty.

When Brink was thirteen, she and three friends spent a summer at her aunt's cabin. During the summer she gathered an intimate knowledge of the cabin's structure and furnishings, the plant life, and a variety of colorful characters moving through the forest. In addition to these personal impressions, Brink meticulously researched information on Gifford Pinchot, the first director of the newly established Forest Service, and on the agency's early history. The struggle between Pinchot and the timber speculators provides the underlying theme for exploring the motives of the assortment of characters who, with the exception of a forest ranger and Pinchot's investigator, were intruders.

Within this particular setting of northern Idaho virgin forests come the inexperienced homesteaders, the packers and residents of the outpost town, timber willies, the young idealist, and the forest ranger. The characters display universal traits of kindness, greed, ambition, selfishness, weakness, and lust. The themes, with the exception of the historical background of the young Forest Service official and his conflict with the homesteaders, are familiar ones. But Brink does provide insights about the position of women at the turn of the century. Even so, this is done within her dichotomy of women who can fit within society and those who reject the rules and become renegades. No new order is created, and without the counterweight of an Anna Hawkins, the male world remains dominant. Yet Brink's espousal of intelligently choosing one's own direction with regard to the lives of others is as forcefully presented here as in *Buffalo Coat*.

Like *Buffalo Coat*, *Strangers in the Forest* is strongly centered on its female protagonists with the theme of inner growth forcefully presented. The heroine of the novel is Meg, a character closely modeled on Brink's Aunt Elsie. She is introduced as irresolute, frivolous, and unprepared for the hard work and isolation in the wilderness. Her passage in the forest is to learn to live on her own without fear.

Here the wilderness shapes character. Meg learns to make her own decisions through the process of creating a home from her small cabin in the clearing. In this pastoral refuge she confronts her greatest fear. During a winter storm, the group of homesteaders lose their way and Meg's feet become frostbitten. After finding Meg's cabin, the others leave her there while they go for help. Fearful that they will not be able to return before she runs out of supplies, she awakes one night. The fire is out and she is petrified by the human-like screams of cougars near the cabin. In these moments Death had approached, and then receded, leaving her with new courage and determination. The experience is like a rebirth, "a thin, clear sense of self-realization which had come to her in the hungry days when she lived with herself alone and faced death as a familiar possibility" (193).

Meg's character is a satisfying portrait for the reader and author who was familiar with this process of growth into a resourceful adulthood. And despite an ending somewhat romantic for modern tastes, Meg emerges as a solid, three-dimensional character of Western literature. She meets her difficulties with resolve, but Brink avoids moving her out of this particular time and place. When Meg realizes that she will lose her claim, she wonders "if she really wanted to do things her own way, or did she want someone to help her find it?" (308).

Meg's antithesis is the beautiful, moody, and strong-willed Lorena, but her character is not so convincingly drawn. The character is probably based on Brink's mother and Aunt Winifred, women that Brink did not fully understand. Brink gives Lorena a childhood of poverty and neglect, and her defense is an aggression carried out to the detriment of those around her. She uses her beauty as a tool to extract the sort of life she feels she is entitled to. But she marries a weak man who cannot indulge her material desires. When she becomes pregnant, Lorena becomes disgusted with her physical appearance. She insists on returning to the homestead cabin for the summer, afraid of being bored in town and left behind by the other homesteaders. There she bears her child with pain and fear, and the infant who is destined to live only five weeks brings a softness to the self-centered woman. Here Brink reveals her sensitivity to the essence of maternity. "She had never wanted a little helpless creature hanging upon her for its livelihood. But, since Ollie had come, her feelings had subtly changed. Ironically now she longed to feed, to nurture, to cherish this baffling, helpless thing, and yet for some reason she could not. Her tears ran down her cheeks, not in anger, but in sorrow and pity for another life, for something outside herself" (232).

Lorena's fate twists through an affair with a French logger, but she also has the resolve to rally the other homesteaders when they learn the government is going to fight them for their homestead claims. Brink selected Lorena over Meg to give an impassioned speech in defense of the homesteaders, and that selection suggests that Brink realized the Anna Hawkins-Meg character had limitations. Lorena steps forward at the meeting, "calm and beautifully poised . . . . 'Men we have trusted have betrayed us. But if my husband won't fight for this place, I will. Who's going to make a home in here, if it isn't the women?" (265).

The male characters in *Strangers in the Forest* serve different purposes. Jeff Carney, the spoiled son of a lumberman, displays a lack of decisiveness and strength of purpose which contrast with the courage and willfulness of his wife, Lorena. His weakness toward his wife and the homesteaders is a good plot for Lorena and his sister Meg, whose strengths take them in opposite directions. His is the most unsympathetic character, and it is not coincidental that the character shares the same occupation and family connection in the novel as did Brink's stepfather, Nat Brown. The two fictional and real characters are not a perfect match, and the discrepancy is probably due as much to literary license as to Brink's later understanding of the motives of this type of man. Toward the end of the novel, Jeff realizes that he has been on the wrong side and that if his son had lived he would have been ashamed of his father (256).

A more interesting and robust male character is the French Canadian lumberjack, Charlie Duporte, modeled on a character Carol had met on her aunt's homestead. Unlike Jeff, Charlie is the resourceful man of the woods, strong, masculine, and handsome. He entertains the homesteaders, particularly Lorena, with his singing and his knowledge of how to survive the hardships of their rustic life. He is endowed with a tenderness and an understanding of women, especially Lorena. He is the one of all the characters who knows how to help Lorena during her childbirth. And at the end of the novel when Jeff has died and Lorena has been badly burned and disfigured by the firestorm of 1910, it is Charlie who takes care of her.

Bundy Jones, the third male protagonist, is the agent who adopts the guise of a botanist when he is dispatched by the Forest Service to investigate the homesteads. He is idealistic, a true follower of Gifford Pinchot and the dream of creating great public forest reserves. Bundy is skeptical of the motives of this odd assortment of people, the "strangers in the forest," especially the women who had little or no knowledge of where they were going or what was required to prove up on a claim. In questioning the presence of these city women in the forest, Bundy also questions whether the timber interests and locators like Jeff Carney could really believe that they could fool the government into giving them the best white pine in the West.

With his training in botany and his mission to save the forests from exploitation, Bundy becomes the spokesman for the beauties of the Western white pine forest. As a youthful and avid observer of nature, Brink was able to skillfully conjure for the reader all the interwoven strands of a particular landscape: the play of light and shadow, fragrances, sounds, and textures. When the homesteaders' pack train enters the valley where they will build their cabins, the presence of the tree—the object of their investment—predominates: "The white pine grows straight and strong with a sturdy masculine upthrust that is suddenly crowned by a feminine delicacy of foliage . . . . Beneath interlocking boughs the sun is filtered away in an unseen sky, leaving a cathedral dimness under high, groined arches" (68).

Strangers in the Forest also explores the human environment of isolation, a common theme of homestead literature. Here it achieves a masterful resonance. On their first trip into their claims, the homesteaders pause at a cabin to deliver mail. Their presence has an unsettling, psychological effect upon the family, the first to settle in the valley. As the man and woman stand in the doorway of the cabin, a small boy runs toward the pack train with an excited greeting and with arms spread in an unconscious gesture of welcome. A man's old overalls, unskillfully cut down to fit him, flap about the boy's thin legs. "The man and woman stood somber in long-held silence, like sleepers disturbed in a dream." It is only when the packer holds up the bundle of mail that they are able to emerge from their sullen dream and begin to smile and talk. The sight of a letter addressed with their own name has "dissolved their paralyzing sense of lonely detachment" (68-69).

Knitting together the vivid personalities, the beauty of nature, and the dramatic plot, is the theme of interlopers in an alien land. They had little reason except profit for embarking on the adventure, and what they pretended to be doing (that is, creating homes and farms) was entirely unsuitable for the type of land they were claiming. The trial in the novel was based upon actual ones. While agreeing with the government's decision to deny the claims, Brink understood the position of some of the homesteaders who indeed had intended to create homes for themselves. Through Meg, Brink balances the opposites of protecting and exploiting the forests. When Meg returns to her cabin after the fire, she finds that the valley has escaped the devastation. She realizes, in an instant's clarity, not only her deep attachment to her land and cabin but also that what she felt was what the government meant about making her claim into a home. Yet as this sensation deepens, so does her foreboding that she will have difficulty convincing the government of her intentions (306-07).

It is characteristic of Brink's personality and life and the times she lived in that the novel is resolved with Meg accepting Bundy's marriage proposal. As she stands in the empty courtroom after the trial realizing that she has lost her claim, Meg admits to herself that she had wanted to do things her own way. Then she had doubts: "But did she, really? Did she really want her own way? Or someone to help her find it?" (308). Her next step of accepting Bundy's offer of marriage was as logical to Brink and to her generation as the unfolding of Brink's own life with her husband.

Reviewers of *Strangers in the Forest* remarked that although the prose and characters were occasionally stilted, the plot was interesting and exciting, and the background vividly drawn (*Booklist*, Oct. 1959). Brink's ability to take the reader into the world of the white pine forests was cited by other reviewers, who agreed that although plausibility was sometimes sacrificed to the story line, the novel was a realistic portrayal of nature in its beauty and power, and it helps the reader appreciate the Idaho pine forests (*Christian Science Monitor* 19 Nov. 1959; *Library Journal* 15 Oct. 1959). Agreeing with the opinions of the reviewers, the *Readers Digest* selected *Strangers* for its series of condensed books.

Brink's third Idaho novel, *Snow in the River*, was her last work of serious fiction and, it could be argued, her best novel. Published in 1964, five years after *Strangers in the Forest*, it reveals a finely tuned sense of self-awareness and balance. In the book she speaks in the first person voice which gives this mixture of history, drama, and autobiography a closeness not found in the two previous novels. Here she was finally able to write down and accept those events which had haunted her throughout her life. Although many writers select the painful events of their early, formative years as themes for a first novel, it is characteristic of Brink's restraint that she waited until late in her life to reveal these most personal events.

Through *Snow in the River*, Brink presents her own emotional growth through the fictional character of Kit. Looking at the adult world through the child's eyes, Brink recaptures the small details of memory that give her writing a distinctive vitality. In the happy, early years, she remembers the prickly green ridges of grass between the bricks, the sensation of sliding down sloping cellar doors, the sound of her mother's piano through the open window, and the white bearskin rug where she played with her dolls listening to her pretty mother's adult conversations. All of these memories were wrapped within the safe, secure world of the pink house her father had built (137-38).

Of all the truths she revealed in the book, none was more terrible than the confession that her mother had never really cared for her. Even the fictional women who shared her mother's traits, such as Lorena in *Strangers in the Forest*, maintained a redeeming warmth of motherhood despite the fickleness of their affections for others. In this book, the mother is distant, even frightening at times to her small daughter. Yet even in the descriptions of quarrels between the mother and stepfather which hint at emotional if not physical abuse, Brink is restrained. The terse prose anticipates the increasing disorder. After her parent's entertainments at the pink house, the house is no longer a haven. One night Kit's mother carries her at night to refuge at her grandmother's house, and the mother's fear goes through Kit like a cold wind (188).

Snow in the River brings together the real and fictional child in a convincing manner consistent with Brink's character. Instead of screaming and fighting against the injustice of her mother's indifference and her own loss, the child withdraws into silence: "It was only in this way that I was able to pull what shreds of resolution I had left about my naked wretchedness" (190).

The funeral is a dividing point between living in a somewhat normal world with parents and families headed by men and living with three women whose financial and social circumstances were much reduced by isolation and penury. The young protagonist, Kit, learns to become self-reliant as she observes the misfortunes accumulating around the surviving family members. She nurtures her inner resources of imagination, reading voraciously and playing with her dolls in a sophisticated new way that would have surprised and worried her grandmother and aunt (210).

In the process of growing up in this unusual family arrangement of grandmother, spinster aunt, and for a time, the presence of her favorite uncle, the fictional Kit sheds more and more of her childhood. Kit's meeting with Uncle Douglas's fianceé, the rich and fascinating widow, does not go well. On the way home for the first time, Kit hides her real thoughts from her uncle and insincerely pronounces Mrs. Rossiter a handsome woman. With this simple lie she helps erect a wall between herself and her beloved uncle, taking her "first step toward adulthood, by aligning myself with the smug and virtuous women against the charming and unvirtuous" (222-23).

Because *Snow in the River* is largely autobiographical, the themes repeated from *Buffalo Coat* and *Strangers in the Forest* are more rounded and understandable. Here the self-centered women

Henrietta and Winifred Watkins assume the roles of Abigail Hedricks and her close friend, Mamie, who has married Alexander's brother, Douglas. Both are unprepared for the responsibilities of marriage and chafe under the strictures of small town society. The character of Abigail is the least well defined. Perhaps because she is the fictional representation of Brink's mother, the author had fewer memories of her. She is portrayed as a beautiful and a skilled musician who prefers the romantic music of Liszt and Tchaikovsky.

Mamie's character is more fully developed and she has a major role in the novel. An impoverished childhood when she took care of her younger siblings has developed her philosophy of life: to be alive and laugh and dance and wear pretty clothes (87). She is determined not to have children but instead to push her husband's ambitions toward a grander life. Both women lack an interest in the conventional family roles of the time. Bored with the daily routines, they amuse themselves with new hats and gossip. Even though Abbie's husband Angus is highly respected in Opportunity, Abbie inwardly fumes at the restraints of her marriage. She appreciates the fact that people trusted and relied upon him, "But what about his wife? Was she to be an old woman before she was thirty?" (134).

Brink criticized this type of woman, but she admitted a fascination with women who dared to act decisively. Mamie returns several years after deserting Douglas to help him through the financial scandal that has driven him into hiding. While she has decided to find Douglas, Kit is unable to follow. She sees her impulses shackled by youth and inexperience and fear, while Mamie is a woman of courage and certainty. "So all my life I have been a prudent Scotswoman, but I have had this vision of recklessness and freedom that I saw one night in Mamie Stephens" (288).

Snow in the River also gave Brink the opportunity to explore sympathetically the character of her Aunt Elsie through the fictional Connie. Connie's father, Dr. Hedrick, forbids her to take up nursing, insisting that it is unsuitable for ladies. He derides her efforts to learn the violin and scorns her for not marrying one of her suitors. It is Angus who perceives that the root of Connie's problems stems from her wanting to feel important, to belong, and that the family has not helped her in that (92). Connie queries Angus, "I think a girl ought to be able to do something for herself, don't you? Do you think it's unladylike to do something besides housekeeping?" (105). Like her real counterpart, the fictional Connie assumes a motherly role to her orphaned niece. In this role she had the disadvantage of being an unmarried woman with a child but without the usual preliminary satisfactions of the flesh (207).

The genius of the book is in using the three Scottish McBain brothers, all with different personalities and expectations, to explore the West of Brink's childhood, the town of Opportunity. The brothers have left behind the poor family croft in Scotland to find a new life, knowing that they may never return. Through their eyes Brink describes this Western town with its unpaved streets, dusty in summer, frozen into ruts in the winter, and with a welter of mud in the spring that forced courting couples to walk out along the railroad tracks (29). Greeting the newly arrived McBain brothers was the boardinghouse, a square frame building with drafty floors and windows that rattled in the wind. But it was "as good as the West afforded in those days and the company it sheltered was young and hopeful. Only the young and hardy came out so far and each man knew that he was on the upgrade" (31).

As guests at Dr. Hedrick's, the McBain brothers marvel at the prodigal meal, but they also notice that the fine house has been thrown together flimsily with wood and shingles instead of the sturdy stone and slate of Scotland. It has the "temporary appearance of a place which expects soon to be supplanted by something finer" (43). Each brother gives us a different perspective on this part of the West. Angus, as the fictional version of Brink's father, becomes the first mayor of Opportunity, is active in the Church, surveys the outlying streets for the expanding town, and in general goes steadily forward in the business of setting the town in order (126). At his death from consumption, his brothers sense a loss of something stable and unchanging, more quiet and honest and upright than most men knew (148).

Willie McBain is carefree, optimistic, and not disposed to take risks in new ventures. He happily settles into his familiar trade of harness maker. Even when bicycles become popular, foreshadowing a new era, he is unable to change the profession he learned as an apprentice in Scotland. His brother Douglas is irritated with someone who would keep on being a saddlemaker in a machine age until the last horse had perished (149).

Douglas McBain, the fictionalized version of Brink's favorite uncle, Donald Ryrie, is a major protagonist. Through his eyes Brink presents a West of unlimited opportunities for the strong and determined. He regards the pristine landscape with calculations of board feet and real estate sales. After working a short period with his brother as an insurance agent for a large company, Douglas enters a real estate partnership with another Scottish immigrant, buys up timberland, and then moves to the regional capital, Manitou City (Spokane). He ultimately loses everything in a speculative scheme to build a dam and irrigation canals in the dry, fertile lands of central Washington. After losing his business, reputation, and wife, he resettles in Seattle. There he admits to Kit, now grown up, that his life has not been successful. "In the end we must have a reckoning and tote up the assets and the debits . . . . you will find Willie living very poorly and cheaply; yet I would like you to know that I know that he has made a greater success of his life than I have made of mine" (308).

While *Snow in the River* may be Brink's strongest novel, it appears to have been dismissed by literary reviewers, although the National League of American Pen Women did give it an award for fiction in 1966. The *New York Times* printed a cursory review, crediting Brink as a fluent but ingenuous storyteller. Indeed, Brink's approach to life as a writer, and arguably as a person, had become outmoded in the 1960s when novels and readers were responding to other writing styles and social concerns. As a writer whose sense of propriety and balance paralleled her personal beliefs, Brink understood that not only the public's appetite for scenes of explicit sex and vice but also its pervasive mood of disillusionment made her writings and perhaps her viewpoints old-fashioned. Sixty-eight at the time *Snow in the River* was published, Brink kept her beliefs, and her writing career slowed.

Her other major work based on her Idaho years is the manuscript "Chain of Hands." Brink submitted it to Macmillan, and when they rejected it, she decided not to pursue other publishers. After her death in 1981, in 1982 her daughter gave the work and publishing rights to the Latah County Historical Society in Moscow.

In 1977 the Latah County Historical Society published *Four Girls on a Homestead*, which Brink had written especially for the organization. This short memoir of her thirteenth summer spent with three high school friends on her aunt's homestead is an excellent example of a reminiscence that avoids being a mere chronicle, and it provides details of this historical period fictionalized in *Strangers in the Forest*. In addition, writing the book and drawing its illustrations brought Brink back to Idaho in a new way. The Historical Society's promotion of this nascent interest in a native author led to a slow but inevitable rediscovery of her as a serious and gifted writer. In 1980 the Society republished *Buffalo Coat* in two printings.

CONNECTIONS WITH OTHER
WESTERN WOMEN AUTHORS

Brink shares with Willa Cather the belief that the land had been exploited by opportunists and that it had disappointed the unrealistic hopes of its pioneers. Both novelists use their female characters to represent a fertile bond with the land while the male characters, notably James Burden in *My Ántonia* and Douglas McBain in *Snow in the River*, turn away from, if not reject, the life connected with tilling the earth. Brink's Dr. Hawkins and Douglas McBain are defeated in their materialistic ambitions, and James Burden discovers how the middle class citizens, absorbed in their business affairs, have lost their feeling for the land (Murphy 55).

Nevertheless, although her fictional townspeople are vulnerable to snobbishness and delight in displaying their wealth, Brink did not suffer Cather's disillusionment with the cultural life in the small towns of the West. Perhaps it was because Brink was able to take advantage of the best her town could offer; perhaps it was the nature of her personality and her grandmother's influence that allowed her to look back at the town and her life there with an objectivity that skirted both bitterness and nostalgia. Perceiving Moscow as a microcosm of life in any large city, Brink saw the pettiness and materialism as no worse than anywhere else.

Like Brink, Mari Sandoz was able to surmount her bitterness toward her domineering and abusive father, a bitterness which dominated the first drafts of *Old Jules* with a "virulence" and "accusatory attitude." Her final effort became a penetrating study of northwestern Nebraska and the symbiotic relationship between Jules and the environment (Stauffer 16-17).

Jean Stafford, unlike Brink and Sandoz, retained a "caustic ambivalence toward the West" (Roberts ix). In the introduction of her collected short stories, published in 1944, she described how she could not wait to quit her "tamed-down native grounds" even though she admitted that her roots remained in the semi-fictitious town of Adams, Colorado (1-2). But Adams lacks the bittersweet, rustic charm of Brink's and Cather's Idaho and Nebraska towns. Adams is ugly with a bandstand in a dreary park, mongrel and multitudinous churches, a high school shaped like a loaf of bread, and the distant oasis of a college campus off limits to two girls who are the main characters. Like the town, they grow up "baffled and mean, like rats in a maze" (283 and 301).

If Brink retained a more positive attitude toward the West, she shared with Cather the knowledge of how it could fail those who believed its resources were unlimited. In *Strangers in the Forest*, Brink set limits, both legal and spiritual, for the exploitation of the great white pine forests. *Snow in the River* shows that it is rainfall and not real estate ventures that determines where agriculture can be profitable. In *Buffalo Coat* the loneliness of the prairies and the hard work defeat the Stevens family, leading to suicide and murder. The Nebraska plains defeat Cather's characters as well. Ántonia's father kills himself, spiritually exhausted by the sod house and his homesickness for Bohemia (*My Ántonia* 101).

Sandoz's depiction in *Old Jules* of the "Kinkaiders," who were unsuited for homesteading claims in the Nebraska sand hills, invites comparisons with Brink's portrayal of the McBains' attempts to set up farms in the arid sagebrush plains of central Washington. The Kinkaiders "were not the homeseekers of the eighties, young, optimistic, eager to battle wind and weather for their land." Instead, they are middle-aged, city-softened, dependent upon railroads and stores, and often without spouse or families (358).

The vitality the immigrant brought to the West is a strong theme in Brink's and Cather's works. Brink nurtured the thrifty Scottish heritage of her father and uncle. Her trip to Scotland soon after the birth of her first child reaffirmed the solid virtues of this heritage, and she takes Douglas McBain back to Scotland when he is a middle-aged man. After a day's hard labor in the fields with his Scottish relatives, Douglas is filled with astonishment that he had once been repulsed by this primitive life. He experiences an unexpected sense of coming home and senses the calm, priceless contentment of his Scottish family who live without strife, rivalry, or dissension (255-56).

Both Brink and Cather were impressed by the resourceful immigrant girls who worked in the houses of the townsfolk. They saw this arrangement as having the possibility of liberating the hired girl from ignorance and dependence on her poor family. The authors interpret this process as a democratic one providing opportunities for these girls to learn English and American customs and to become ladies by marrying well or to set up their own businesses. Cather contrasts the robustness and spiritual vitality of the Czech girls to the listless and dull daughters of the local merchants who were convinced that they were "refined" (199).

Brink and Cather also perceive that the connection between hired girl and mistress could obliterate social differences in Western towns where the new middle class might be only one step ahead of the immigrants. In *My Ántonia*, Ántonia and her mistress Mrs. Harling, who share "strong, independent natures," enjoy a "basic harmony," both knowing what they like and not trying to imitate other people (180). In *Buffalo Coat*, Anna and the hired Swedish girl become friends and companions, to the distress of Dr. Hawkins, who would prefer his wife to socialize with the local elite. When Lena leaves the Hawkins household to marry a Swedish farmer, she has assimilated what she needs to become accepted into "respectable" society.

NON-IDAHO WORKS

The three Idaho novels represent a small portion of Carol Brink's total of twenty-seven books. Brink wrote most of her adult fiction and non-fiction works from the mid-1940s when *Buffalo Coat* was published to the mid-1960s when she completed *Snow in the River*. During these years Brink was in her late forties to her sixties, not surprising for a woman whose primary duties in the preceding years were devoted to her children. The delay in her writing career also afforded her a more mature perspective on marriage, family life, and the larger world.

After writing *Buffalo Coat*, Brink turned to a biography of the Hutchinson family of Massachusetts and New Hampshire. Set in the mid-1800s, *Harps in the Wind* (1947) is the chronicle of this famous singing family. Departing from the familiar territory of Idaho and home town characters, Brink embarked on extensive research into the family and the historical background of New England. A compelling reason for this undertaking was her life-long interest in racial tolerance, liberty, international peace, and the brotherhood of man, causes which the Hutchinsons promoted through their songs. Although *Harps in the Wind* is not the peer of the Idaho novels, the reviewers praised Brink's narrative skill and ability to create atmosphere (*Chicago Sun Book Week* 23 March 1947).

Stopover (1951) sprang from Brink's fascination with the question of individual freedom versus responsibility. The novel combines the Midwestern setting of a small university town with characters drawn from *Buffalo Coat*. Although Brink roundly denied the connection, the main female character, Naomi Murdoch, is clearly based on her aunt, Winifred Watkins. In *Stopover* Brink was characteristically able to view the fictionalized Winifred with sympathy.

As the critics pointed out, the theme of *Stopover* was hardly original: a second-rate actress who deserted her older husband and three children for a stage career returns to her hometown. Naomi, like Mamie in *Snow in the River*, suffered a brutal childhood, and her marriage to a high school teacher stifled her high spirits and ambitions. After a short love affair with a forceful man—a hunter and proprietor of a local saloon—she precipitately left town. Ten years later after receiving an invitation from her daughter Lily to attend Lily's high school graduation and performance in the school play, Naomi impulsively returns.

Naomi is the antithesis of the solid women in Brink's life, yet her actions are interpreted as more ingenuous and selfish than calculated to harm. Most of Naomi's intentions are good-natured but she is easily bored by routine. Through this character Brink explores the reasons for a woman to desert her family, whether by suicide or by running away. Naomi admits that she has just loved too many things. Naomi possesses another quality that Brink admires, that of courage and the ability to make and act out decisions. Yet the courage Naomi possesses, like Mamie's, is fatally flawed because of the harm it does others.

Challenging Naomi is her daughter Joyce, who suffers the pain and disgrace of her mother's disappearance. Like the adolescent Brink, Joyce finds herself unable to forgive her mother; and through Joyce, Brink reveals the inner torment of her own youth. "Early in life, when most girls were soft in their mothers' hands, Joyce had been forced into mature judgments and opinions . . . . Yet she had a kind of shyness, too, the shyness of the extremely conscious person who has suffered a hurt and holds a protecting hand before the wound" (14).

The critics' reactions to *Stopover* were mixed. *Catholic World* not unexpectedly called it a preposterous book; others recommended it as a good story, well-written, and serving as well-integrated propaganda for order versus confusion and for the acceptance of social responsibility. Despite an empathy with the reckless and selfish people in this book, Brink stops short of fully exploring the darker underside of her renegade characters.

Some of Carol Brink's favorite memories sprang from the times she spent in France during her husband's sabbaticals. The transformation of these experiences into fiction had mixed results in *The Headland* (1955). Her insights into the world of childhood misled her in this novel. The story follows a group of children to maturity amid the devastation of World War II, revealing many fine details of French culture.

The characters are a mixture of nationalities with predictable traits: wild, bold, and freedom-loving Americans; emotional and proud Spaniards; and the restrained English girl. The description of a special community these children establish is believable, but the theme of individuality versus social responsibility does not mesh comfortably with the political background of occupied France. One reason may be a lack of knowledge of the historical period, and the novel presents a somewhat superficial dramatization of complicated moral and political issues. One critic pronounced this a "pleasant tale, without profound significance" (*Kirkus* 15 July 1955). Others praised the author's warmth and her grace and sensitivity in depicting the childhood experiences (*Library Journal* Aug. 1955).

In the *Chateau Saint Barnabé* (1963), Brink's ability to capture the essence of French culture is right on the mark. This reminiscence of her family's stay in the south of France in 1924 is a small gem. It sparkles with the author's keen observations of French life while retaining the fresh and honest perspective of an American writer and mother. The Brinks spent only five weeks in the chateau, but she found that this short period possessed a wholeness, "a complete experience with beginning, climax and ending, rounded at the corners like a poem or short story." There are no complicated plots or flamboyant characters to manipulate, and the result is a vivid portrait, wonderfully dramatic and real.

Not only in *Chateau* but also in *The Twin Cities*, Brink beautifully combines the genre of travel literature with family and personal reminiscences. She reluctantly undertook the task of writing a guide to St. Paul and Minneapolis. It was published in 1961 as part of a planned series on the cities of America. Brink agreed to the project on the condition that she could do it in her own way. Macmillan enthusiastically accepted her terms and agreed that they wanted a "person kind of thing" and not a standard guidebook (Interview Tapes 4 and 14).

As a writer who preferred writing from memory and emotions, Brink found the research exceedingly tedious. Yet the book is well-crafted, and the combination of factual information with the author's observations as a longtime resident serves to give us an excellent guide to the history and contemporary life, culture, and industry of these two cities. Brink's personal viewpoint is refreshing, bringing to life what could have been a predictable guidebook approach. Brink introduces the region through the eyes of a young woman recently arrived from rural Idaho. Her first view of the Mississippi is disappointing, "Was this gentle stream the mighty river? I could not even tell which way it was flowing" (1).

Brink's childhood curiosity about immigrants who settled in Idaho is matched by her adult interest in those who settled in Minnesota. She notes the mixture of nationalities, why some have assimilated and others have not, and the reason Scandinavians chose this region which reminded them of their homes. Brink was not unaware of racial problems, although by today's criteria her remarks appear somewhat innocent. She does deserve credit for addressing the subject in a book intended as pleasant reading: "Negroes are in a minority and we get along well with them. But, if they made up half of our population, would the rest of us be so

46

tolerant?" (82).

In 1976 Bantam Books published Brink's *The Bellini Look*, a gothic romance set in Venice. Although done as a light-hearted literary adventure, it is entirely engrossing as a mystery and romance with a solid plot and lyrical descriptions of people and places Brink knew well from her travels in Italy.

BRINK'S PLACE IN REGIONAL LITERATURE

In ranking Brink with other Idaho and regional writers, it is apparent that she has not received the recognition she deserves even in view of the uneven quality of her works. As yet there exists no critical examination of her work. Correspondence, personal papers, and other biographical materials still remain to be collected and perused.

The lack of attention to Brink is undoubtedly due to her reputation as a children's writer. Although writers and critics may agree on the importance of good fiction for children and the difficulty of producing it, they do not perceive these authors as being "serious writers" with a status equal to the creators of adult books. Writing for children is viewed as a hobby, one that serious writers avoid. From this perspective, winning the Newbery Award early in her career was both a blessing and a hindrance.

Another reason for a lack of recognition is the nature of her writings. Her books are well-crafted and intriguing, but they generally do not lead us to new visions or interpretations of life. They can instruct us, move us, and entertain us. But they do not shock us. Neither does Brink's life. She is neither glamorous nor rebellious. Yet Brink's writings give us insight into the strengths and foibles of human beings. Even though she adheres to the old-fashioned virtues, she retains an empathy with her characters in spite of their flaws. Although Brink avoids vulgarity and sordidness, she reflects openly on the consequences of a society losing not only its sense of morality but also self-discipline, honor, and wisdom.

Selected Bibliography

WORKS BY BRINK

ADULT FICTION

Buffalo Coat. New York: Macmillan, 1944.

Harps in the Wind. New York: Macmillan, 1947.

Stopover. New York: Macmillan, 1951.

The Headland. New York: Macmillan, 1955.

Strangers in the Forest. New York: Macmillan, 1959.

The Twin Cities. New York: Macmillan, 1961.

Chateau Saint Barnabé. New York: Macmillan, 1962.

Snow in the River. New York: Macmillan, 1964.

The Bellini Look. Des Plaines, IL: Bantam, 1976.

JUVENILE FICTION

Anything Can Happen on the River. New York: Macmillan, 1934.

Caddie Woodlawn. New York: Macmillan, 1935.

Mademoiselle Misfortune. New York: Macmillan, 1936.

Baby Island. New York: Macmillan, 1937.

All Over Town. New York: Macmillan, 1939.

Lad with a Whistle. New York: Macmillan, 1941.

Magical Melons. New York: Macmillan, 1944.

Caddie Woodlawn, A Play. New York: Macmillan, 1945.

Narcissa Whitman. New York: Row, 1945.

Lafayette. New York: Row, 1946.

Minty et Compagnie. Dronten, The Netherlands: Casterman Nederland, 1945.

Family Grandstand. New York: Viking, 1952.

The Highly Trained Dogs of Professor Petit. New York: Macmillan, 1953.

Family Sabbatical. New York: Viking, 1956.

The Pink Motel. New York: Macmillan, 1945.

Andy Buckram's Tin Men. New York: Macmillan, 1966.

Winter Cottage. New York: Macmillan, 1968.

Two Are Better Than One. New York: Macmillan, 1968.

MISCELLANEOUS WORKS AND INTERVIEWS

"A Chain of Hands," manuscript at Latah County Historical Society, Moscow, Idaho, c. 1970.

Rags and Patches, poetry, self-published, n.d.

"Keep the Bough Green." *Horn Book* (1967): 447-53.

"The Gold Mine of Experience." *The Writer* Aug. 1977: 11-14.

Interview with questions from Sam Schrager. Latah County Historical Society. Transcribed. 1976.

Interviews by Mary Reed. Latah County Historical Society. Transcribed. July 1981.

WORKS CITED AND OTHER SECONDARY SOURCES

Attebery, Louie. "Another Look at Caddie Woodlawn." Paper presented in July 1990; a copy of the paper is at the Latah County Historical Society, Moscow, Idaho.

Bullock, Florence Haxton. "Mama Never Repented." *New York Herald Tribune Weekly Book Review* 18 Mar. 1951: 12.

Cather, Willa. *My Ántonia*. Boston: Houghton, 1961.

_____. *Early Novels and Stories*. New York: Library of America, 1987.

Commire, Anne, ed. *Something About the Author*. Vol. 1. Detroit: Gale, 1971. 34-35.

Drury, John. "A Famous Pioneer Family of Singers." *Chicago Sun Book Week* 23 Mar. 1947: 9.

Gaither, Frances. "Round-Trip Prodigal." *Saturday Review of Literature* 10 Mar. 1951: 15.

_____. "The Past Recaptured." *New York Times Book Review* 2 Oct. 1955: 32.

Holbrook, Stewart H. "The Singing Hutchinsons." *New York Herald Tribune Weekly Book Review* 6 Apr. 1947: 8.

Hughes, Riley. "Review." *Catholic World* 1 Jan. 1959: 312-13.

Murphy, John J. "Willa Cather." *Fifty Western Writers: A Bio-Bibliographical Sourcebook*. Ed. Fred Erisman and Richard W. Etulain. Westport, CT: Greenwood, 1982. 51-62.

Purtell, Thelma. "Sad Symbol." *New York Times Book Review* 26 Nov. 1944: 18.

Reed, Mary E. "Folklore in Regional Literature: Carol Brink's *Buffalo Coat*." *Idaho Folklife: Homesteads to Headstones*. Ed. Louie Attebery. Salt Lake City: U of Utah P and the Idaho State Historical Society, 1985. 216-22.

Roberts, David. *Jean Stafford: A Biography*. Boston: Little, 1988.

Sandoz, Mari. *Old Jules*. Boston: Little, 1935.

Simonds, Katherine. "Ironic Opportunity." *Saturday Review of Literature* 2 Dec. 1944: 56.

Stafford, Jean. *The Collected Stories of Jean Stafford*. New York: Farrar, 1969.

Stauffer, Helen Winter. *Mari Sandoz*. Western Writers Series 63. Boise: Boise State U, 1984.

Taylor, J. Golden, Editor-in-Chief; Thomas J. Lyon, Senior Editor. *A Literary History of the American West*. Fort Worth: Texas Christian UP, 1987.

WESTERN WRITERS SERIES

This continuing series, primarily regional in nature, provides brief but authoritative introductions to the lives and works of authors who have written significant literature about the American West. These attractive, uniform fifty-page pamphlets are useful to the general reader as well as to teachers and students.

Please send orders to: Business Manager   Boise State University
                        BSU Western Writers Series   Boise, Idaho 83725
                        English Department

DEPARTMENT OF ENGLISH
BOISE STATE UNIVERSITY
BOISE, IDAHO 83725

WESTERN WRITERS SERIES

(list continued on inside of back cover)

Please send orders to: Business Manager
BSU Western Writers Series
English Department

Boise State University
Boise, Idaho 83725